This book belongs to:

____

Made in the USA
Monee, IL
07 July 2026

56552286R00066